Mathematical Minds

A Guide to Assessing Attainment Target One

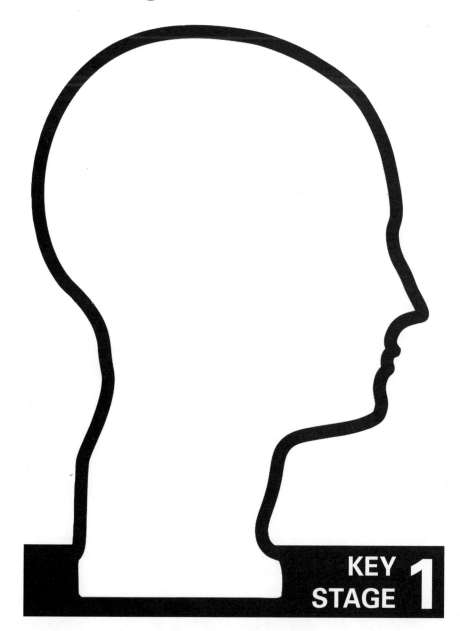

KEY STAGE 1

Joanne Morris
National Foundation for Educational Research

Published by nferNelson Publishing Company Ltd
The Chiswick Centre
414 Chiswick High Road
London W4 5TF, UK

www.nfer-nelson.co.uk

nferNelson is a division of Granada Learning Limited, part of Granada plc.

© NFER-NELSON, 2003

All curriculum references are taken from:
Department for Education and Employment and Qualifications and Curriculum Authority (1999) *The National Curriculum for England: Key Stages 1–4*. London: HMSO.

All rights reserved, including translation. Except where otherwise indicated, no part of this publication may be reproduced or transmitted in any form or by any means, electronic or mechanical, including photocopying, recording or duplication in any information storage and retrieval system, without permission in writing from the publishers and may not be photocopied or otherwise reproduced even within the terms of any licence granted by the Copyright Licensing Agency.

Photocopying restrictions
Photocopying restrictions will be waived on certain pages within this publication, indicated by the inclusion of this symbol, on full payment of the invoice accompanying it. This is intended to aid you in the effective use of the materials within your organisation. Until full payment is received, all photocopying restrictions remain in force and any photocopying is illegal.

Once the book has been purchased, please note that:

a) All other copyright restrictions remain in force.
b) Photocopies may only be made for use *within* the purchaser's school, department or other organisation. Photocopies may not be made for distribution to other organisations. In particular, the waiving of photocopying restrictions does *not* cover this book's use in surveys or large-scale research projects.

If you have any doubts about your use of the photocopiable material in this book, please telephone nferNelson and ask for the Contracts Manager.

Typesetting by Oxford Designers & Illustrators
Printed by Thanet Press, Margate, Kent

Code 0090008637   ISBN 0 7087 03682   1(02.03)

Contents

Acknowledgements v

Introduction 1

Delivery time 2

Gnome homes 6

Number puzzles 10

Sending a letter 14

The new front door 20

Mathematics levels for Attainment target 1 25

Acknowledgements

We would like to thank all the schools that gave us permission to try out these activities, and all the teachers and pupils in these schools who took part in the activities and provided samples of work.

(Please note that the spelling and grammar in the examples of pupils' work has not been corrected.)

Introduction

This book describes techniques that can help you assess pupils' performance in Attainment Target 1 (AT1). After you have used the activities in this book, you should find that you are able to see opportunities for assessing AT1 during other class activities, with little or no adaptation of tasks or interruption of learning.

Each section of this book:
- describes an activity;
- links to the National Curriculum Programme of Study (e.g. Ma2/1f);
- gives guidance on how to assess pupils' performance;
- discusses samples of pupils' work.

The aim is to give you ideas about how assessment of AT1 can be carried out in class during activities that are useful and interesting for pupils, and to help you use the results of assessment to further develop pupils' skills.

In some cases, you may choose to assess one pupil or a small group by observing them while they work and by asking questions, while at other times you may wish to assess the whole class by, for example, asking them to produce a written record that can be marked.

When using the activities in this book, the following points should be borne in mind:

- Assessment objectives are given for each activity. These summarise the areas in which pupils will have opportunities to demonstrate their skills. However, you will not necessarily either want or be able to assess all these areas in the course of one activity. You may choose to focus on one in particular if you are assessing a large number of pupils or, if assessing an individual or a small group, you may be able to use observation and questioning to assess a wider range of skills.

- The nature of the skills being assessed means that you need to step back from what pupils are doing and allow them to solve their own problems and come to their own conclusions as much as possible. If you find that you have to give help and support, try prompting the pupil to solve the problem first. You will need to take into account during assessment the amount of support needed, since the ability to work independently, think for oneself and work out solutions is an important aspect of AT1.

- In some cases, pupils need to have particular subject knowledge to be able to successfully complete an activity. If you want to focus on assessment of AT1, you will need to be sure that the activity is within the scope of what pupils have previously learnt. Otherwise, pupils may not be able to demonstrate the specific skills which you want to assess. Remember that your aim is not to assess knowledge or understanding in other areas, only in AT1.

- General guidance is given about the levels of attainment that can be identified for the samples of pupil performance in each activity. This does not necessarily imply that the pupil is definitely at this level – rather that this particular observation or piece of work can be judged to be evidence of work at this level. To build up a definite judgment of a pupil's level in AT1, you would need to gather evidence from a wider range of work.

- For convenience, the levels for AT1 are described on page 25.

Activity

Delivery time

MATHEMATICAL CONTEXT

Ma3 Shape, space and measures
- Estimating the size and order of objects by direct comparison using appropriate language (Ma3/4a).
- Comparing and measuring objects using uniform non-standard units (for example, a straw, wooden cubes), then with a standard unit of length (cm) (Ma3/4a).

ASSESSMENT OBJECTIVES

During this task, you may be able to observe whether the pupils can:

Problem solving
- try different approaches and find ways of overcoming difficulties when solving shape and space problems (Ma3/1a);
- select and use appropriate mathematical equipment when solving problems involving measures or measurement (Ma3/1b);

Communicating
- use the correct language and vocabulary for shape, space and measures (Ma3/1d);

Reasoning
- recognise simple spatial patterns and relationships and make predictions about them (Ma3/1e);
- use mathematical communication and explanation skills (Ma3/1f).

Materials needed
- A simple map, one for each pupil, such as the one shown on page 5 (which may be photocopied)
- A selection of coloured pencils
- A selection of equipment for measuring including standard and non-standard measures (e.g. rulers, string, multi-link cubes, paperclips, etc.)

A brief outline
Pupils use strategies to predict and discover which route on a map will be the shortest.

The activity

1 Introduce the task

Explain that Bob's Bakery delivers bread every morning to Food2Go supermarket. A new driver has started and he does not know which way to go. Bob the Baker has given him a map. The pupils have to show on the map all the different routes he could take to the shop and find out which route would be the *shortest*.

2 Work through the task
- Having explained the task to the pupils, you may then wish to ask the pupils how many different routes there might be and how they can show all the different routes on one map.
- Encourage each pupil to find at least three or four routes.

- Observe the pupils as they work and discuss their work with them as you feel appropriate. Some pupils may need prompting when thinking about how to measure the routes, but encourage them to be as independent as possible and note any support given.

Guidance on assessment and examples of pupils' work

Pupils originally worked with coloured pencils for this activity. Colour has been replaced by shading and different line styles in the pupils' work presented in this book.

Example 1: Helena

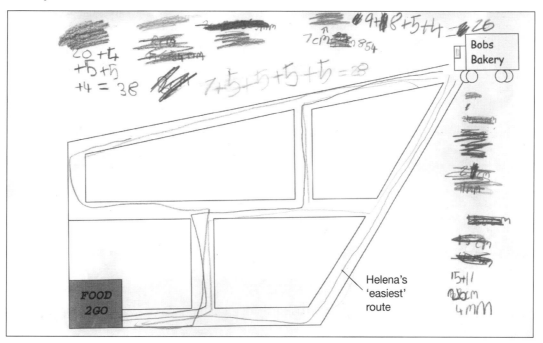

Helena adopted a strategy being employed by a peer, which was to use coloured lines to draw each route.

In the same way as most of the group, Helena chose a ruler to measure her routes but became confused when reading off measurements. She considered a range of resources that had been made available for the task, including non-standard alternatives. However, she was keen to continue working with a ruler, asking for assistance to read the measurements. First she measured what she thought was *'the easiest route'* (shown above). A degree of inaccuracy crept into her work as she began to measure the printed road lines rather than the coloured lines she had drawn herself. When asked if she thought it mattered which measurement she took, her reply indicated that she was not aware of the potential for any error.

As she worked, Helena made running calculations in her head and on her piece of paper, but often became lost and confused (hence the crossings out). She chose colours randomly for recording her measurements. These did not correspond to the colours which she had used to draw the routes, so she became confused when trying to match the calculation to a particular route. She went back and assigned shading and arrows to help give her written work more clarity, but this did not correspond to her oral explanations.

Helena was surprised, but quite pleased, to find that two of her marked routes measured the same (26cm). When asked which one she thought would be better for the driver, she suggested the same route as the one she had identified as the easiest because it was *'straighter, it would be hard to get lost. With the other one you have to turn a couple of times and you might have to wait.'*

In working on this task, Helena was able to select appropriate aspects of her mathematical skills and knowledge. She usefully and appropriately employed her addition and measuring skills although, in both instances, her workings were not entirely secure or accurate. Her knowledge of standard units of measurement seemed rather fragile but she chose to persist with them rather than work with non-standard units. She was able to use appropriate vocabulary such as 'shortest', 'longest' and 'least' in discussing her work. Helena often confused herself while writing things down and did not yet bring any independent organisational skills to her work. The understanding, reasoning and problem-solving skills that were conveyed through discussion of this task were deemed to show some evidence of work at Level 2 in AT1. However, this was not reflected in Helena's written workings, so there is not enough evidence of secure Level 2 performance in this task.

Example 2: Gavin

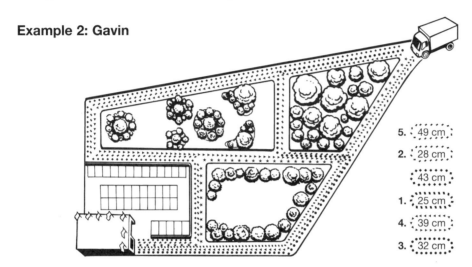

Before he began working, Gavin predicted which route he thought would be the shortest. He asked if he could get some coloured pencils so that he could use a different colour to define each possible route. First he drew all the possible routes he could see and then set about measuring them.

Gavin attempted to measure his lines with a ruler, but struggled as the lines were not very straight. He commented that this method would be *'about right'*. He seemed to recognise there was a margin of error in this method, but thought that it was suitable for the task as it did not demand specific measurements. When asked what he would do if two measurements were similar, he suggested he would *'check them with some string and then measure the string'*.

Gavin recorded each route as he measured it, noting the length of each section orally and keeping a running total in his head. He listed the total measurement for each route in sequence of measurement, using appropriate colour coding. After this, unprompted, he went back and ranked the measurements *'in order, from shortest to longest'*. He was pleased that his prediction had been proved correct.

In this piece of work, Gavin demonstrated elements of both Levels 2 and 3 in AT1. He anticipated the problems arising from drawing all possible routes in pencil, so adopted the practice of using colour to define different routes. He also identified the potential need to use alternative and appropriate equipment to resolve any further difficulties. He was able to discuss his work using subject-appropriate vocabulary. Gavin organised his work to some extent (e.g. rank ordering of measurements), but did not to check his work carefully – he did not re-measure any of his routes and missed one out in his rank ordering.

Pupil worksheet

Date:

Name:

Class:

Map

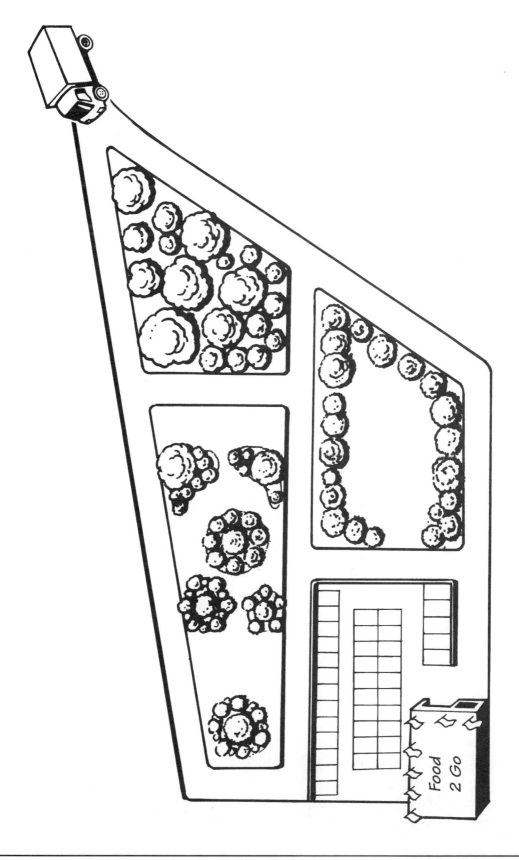

Activity

Gnome homes

MATHEMATICAL CONTEXT

Ma3 Shape, space and measures
- Describing properties of shapes that pupils can see using the related vocabulary (Ma3/2a).
- Creating 2-D shapes and 3-D shapes (Ma3/2c).
- Recognising reflective symmetry in familiar 2-D shapes and patterns (Ma3/2d).

ASSESSMENT OBJECTIVES

During this task, you may be able to observe whether the pupils can:

Problem solving
- try different approaches and find ways of overcoming difficulties when solving shape and space problems (Ma3/1a);

Communicating
- use the correct language and vocabulary for shape (Ma3/1d);

Reasoning
- recognise simple spatial patterns and relationships and make predictions about them (Ma3/1e);
- use mathematical communication and explanation skills (Ma3/1f).

Materials needed
- Plenty of multi-link cubes for each pupil

A brief outline
Pupils investigate the number of shapes they can make with four multi-link cubes, and discuss their observations.

The activity

1 Introduce the task

Explain that the pupils are going to help design some new homes for gnomes. The King of the Gnomes has given each gnome in Gnomeland four cubes to build a new home. Obviously, the gnomes all want their houses to be different to their neighbours'. The pupils are to use the multi-link cubes to build some different gnome homes. Pupils must remember to use *four cubes* for each home.

2 Work through the task

- Having explained the task, remind the pupils that they can only have four cubes for any one shape.
- Suggest that they keep the shapes they make as they go along. (This may lead to some interesting discussions about whether shapes are the same or different if pupils begin to notice reflections and rotations.)
- Observe the pupils as they work and discuss their work with them as you feel appropriate. Make a note of any discussions the pupils have or explanations they give while they work.

- If pupils become stuck after making a series of shapes that are one cube high, you may wish to prompt them with appropriate questions that lead them on to consider shapes that are two, three or four cubes high. Note any prompts given.

Guidance on assessment and examples of pupils' work

Example 1: Cameron

Cameron worked steadily to produce several different gnome homes. He worked carefully and independently, choosing not to discuss his work with other group members. As he began to make each shape, he collected up four cubes and put them together, checking against the ones he had already made that the one he was creating was novel.

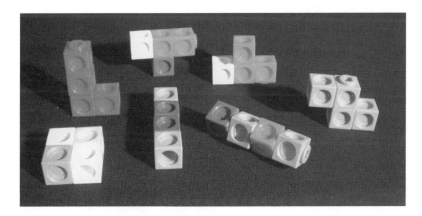

The shapes Cameron produced were generally varied apart from the T-shape and inverted T-shape (shown top middle of the photograph above). When asked, he did not make any connection between these two shapes. When requested to talk about the shapes he had made, he said: *'They're all made of four cubes'*. When asked about particular methods for making the shapes he replied: *'I just put them together each time'*.

Cameron approached the task in a straightforward way. He did not seem to be aware of relationships between the shapes he was making or have any particular system in place to investigate the possibilities. The vocabulary used in discussion of the task was appropriate though rather limited. He was judged to demonstrate aspects of Level 1 performance in AT1 in this activity.

Example 2: Finn, Grace and Bradley

These three pupils all settled to the task with much enthusiasm and worked independently. However, before long, discussion began spontaneously about their work both in terms of how they were going about the task and the resulting products.

Bradley began by questioning two of the shapes he had made (see below): *'Are they the same?'* He concluded that:

'If I put them this way, then they're the same.'

'But I can put them like this and then they're different.'

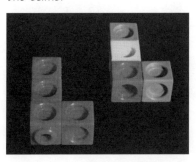
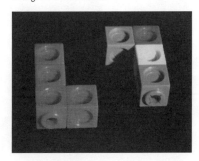

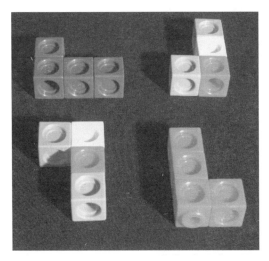

He later went on to expand this idea, producing the set pictured here.

Bradley made a wide range of shapes, commenting to his peers on the method he employed: '... *making the same shape each time to start with, then moving cubes and taking them apart to make a different shape*'. He discussed his work using appropriate positional and shape vocabulary but also drew parallels with his environment, commenting that one of his shapes looked '*like a climbing frame*'.

Bradley was judged to be working at Level 2 in AT1 on this particular activity.

Finn took great pride in the number of gnome homes he had generated and was observed to establish several criteria which, in his mind, denoted difference between shapes.

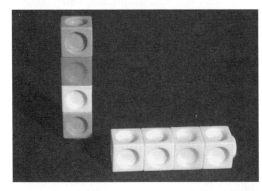

When asked if these shapes were two different shapes he replied: '*Yes, because that one's tall and that one's long so they're different*'.

Through further observation and conversation it became evident that he had then slightly modified this idea to create a criterion of '*flat or tall*', as demonstrated by this picture.

Mathematical Minds Key Stage 1

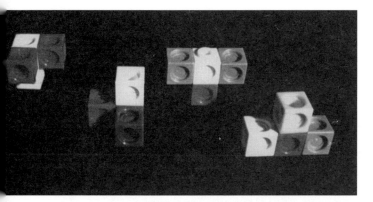

Finn also used 'inversion' as a criterion, as shown in this collection of gnome homes.

When Bradley was discussing similarities and differences in his L-shapes (see discussion on page 7), Finn likened this to the T-shapes and inverted T-shapes that he had made, and reached the same conclusion – by inverting the shape he could produce a different one.

While he did not always make his criteria or rules explicit, watching Finn work made it clear that this was the way he was thinking. He was actively seen to replicate a shape and then invert it to create another 'home'. He was also demonstrating use of reflection and rotation of shapes, but did not seem to be aware of this. When specifically asked, Finn was aware of some of his methods (as demonstrated in an earlier discussion), but not all. However, his exploration was beginning to show a systematic and methodical approach.

Finn's work in this activity was judged to demonstrate some elements of Level 3 in AT1. He developed a range of criteria that were very effective as approaches to solving the task, though some of these appeared to be on a subconscious level. He was starting to adopt a systematic approach and organised method in his work. Finn was able to discuss his work and explain his thinking although, to be more secure in Level 3, his vocabulary needed to be more mathematically specific and sophisticated.

After working for a while, **Grace** noticed that she could make *'different shapes'* by rotating and reflecting the ones she had already made, so she began work to increase her collection. She made a 2 by 2 by 1 cuboid then, recognising that she had that shape already, rotated half of it through 90°. She was pleased to realise she had made another shape and was keen to show the rest of the group how she had discovered it.

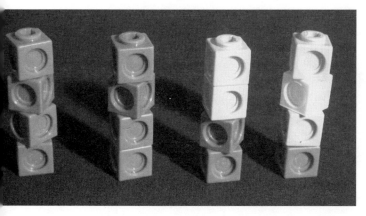

Just when she thought she had exhausted her efforts, Grace came up with the idea of twisting the bottom cube of a vertical column: *'Look, that's different because instead of having all flat faces, the one at the bottom has a corner sticking out'*. She then decided that she could continue this series by having the 'twisted cube' in a different position in the column each time, and also by having more than one cube twisted.

It was clear from her actions that Grace was beginning to understand that, by moving individual cubes within the basic shapes, she could make an almost infinite number of new shapes. However, she was not yet able to express this.

Grace used a good range of appropriate mathematical vocabulary while discussing her work and made use of innovative approaches in this task. She was beginning to work systematically. Time constraints meant that she was not able to develop the challenge as fully as she might have done. However, it was felt that the work she produced on this task showed some good mathematical thinking and was securely within Level 3 in AT1.

Activity

Number puzzles

MATHEMATICAL CONTEXT

Ma2 Number

- Understanding addition and using related vocabulary; recognising that addition can be done in any order (Ma2/3a).
- Understanding subtraction as both 'take away' and 'difference' and using the related vocabulary (Ma2/3a).
- Recording calculations in a number sentence, using the symbols +, – and = correctly (Ma2/3e).
- Choosing sensible calculation methods to solve whole-number problems, drawing on their understanding of the operations (Ma2/4a).
- Checking that their answers are reasonable and explaining their methods or reasoning (Ma2/4b).

ASSESSMENT OBJECTIVES

During this task, you may be able to observe whether the pupils can:

Problem solving
- approach problems involving number in order to identify what they need to do (Ma2/1a);
- develop flexible approaches to problem solving and look for ways to overcome difficulties (Ma2/1b);
- make decisions about which operations and problem-solving strategies to use (Ma2/1c);
- organise and check their work (Ma2/1d);

Communicating
- use the correct language, symbols and vocabulary associated with number (Ma2/1e);
- communicate in spoken and written form, using mathematical language and symbols (Ma2/1f);

Reasoning
- present results in an organised way (Ma2/1g);
- explain their methods and reasoning when solving problems involving number (Ma2/1i).

Materials needed
- Practical aids (if required) such as magnetic numbers and symbols, number and symbol cards, objects to count, number squares
- Pencil and paper or access to another suitable method of recording
- Each pupil's three given numbers

A brief outline

Given three numbers, pupils use addition and subtraction to generate as many totals as they can.

The activity

1 Introduce the task

Explain that you are going to give each pupil three numbers (e.g. 1, 3 and 4). The pupils must use their numbers and the symbols +, − and = to make up some number sentences/stories (use phraseology that pupils are used to). Then they record all the different totals they can make using only their three numbers and symbols. You may wish to give the pupils different sets of numbers which are appropriately matched to their number ability (this will also promote independent work within the group).

2 Work through the task

- Having explained the task to the pupils, encourage each of them to find as many different totals as they can. There should be no limit on the number of times they use each number or even each symbol, leaving the investigation as open-ended as the individual cares to make it. You may wish to encourage pupils to find at least 12 totals (depending on their pace of work).

- Observe the pupils as they work and discuss their work with them, as you feel appropriate. Encourage the pupils to be as independent as possible and note any support given.

- After the pupil has finished, invite them to explain any systems they used to work through different operations to discover totals.

Guidance on assessment and examples of pupils' work

Example 1: Hamish

Hamish worked quickly to create this list of sums and totals, then claimed he could not *'think of any more'*. He was asked if he had checked his work and said that he had. He was happy to use both the operation of subtraction and of addition, though his responses to later subtraction sums suggested he was not yet secure in his understanding and application of this operation. He was not as thorough in his subtraction work as in his addition work.

The presentation of his work was simple but clear. However, although Hamish appeared to have understood the task, his presentation of the totals at the bottom of the page suggested he had forgotten that he had been asked how many *different* totals he could find. He demonstrated minimal perseverance skills in this activity, adopting a brief

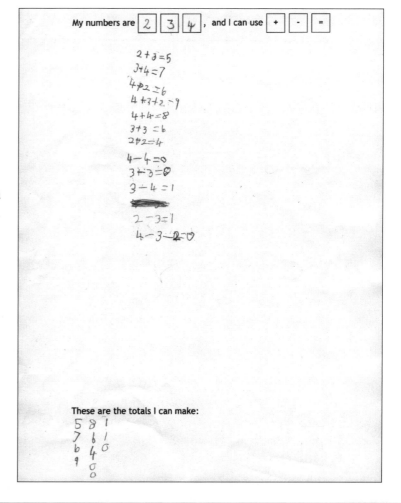

straightforward simplistic approach to the task, and did not seek to develop it in any way. He used simple patterns and relationships to create a number of sums, some of which shared the same total. Hamish was able to use the language of addition and subtraction in discussing his work and used numbers and symbols appropriately to show his workings.

Hamish's skills in subtraction and checking the accuracy of his work have yet to be developed to an appropriate level. He showed some elements of Levels 1 and 2 in AT1 in this piece of work. What he did was, on the whole, done well; but his overall achievement was rather limited. To show secure Level 2 attainment, he would need to be more consistent in the checking of his work and in his ability to explore, broaden and develop problem-solving approaches.

Example 2: Erin

After the task was introduced, Erin asked: *'Can you use plus and minus together in the same sum?'* to further define her work. She also took on board the response to another pupil's question, which was whether all the numbers could be used at the same time. She developed this a step further by asking if she could *'use two of the numbers together like 2 and 5 to be 25'*. Erin began working and, as the first few sums show, she experimented with the freedom of the task rather than adopting a systematic approach. She numbered each sum and pointed out that she was putting a full stop as a separator between number and sum *'so that you don't think that number is part of the sum'*.

Erin paused after the seventh sum $4 + 3 = 7$. It was then suggested to her that she could now go on to do $3 + 4$. However, she pointed out that *'that wouldn't be any good because it makes 7'*. When asked why it would not be any good she replied: *'because it's the same answer and I have to find as many different ones as I can'*.

Erin worked very confidently with numbers and, as the numbers with which she was dealing became larger, she made effective and accurate use of a number square to support her addition skills. She tended to rely on addition rather than subtraction. This reluctance may suggest that she is not yet as secure in her understanding and application of subtraction.

On reaching the repeated addition of 23 (see sum 19), Erin became lost after adding together the first two or three lots of 23, and became frustrated about not knowing which instance of 23 she had already included and which she had not. *'I know'*, she said, and went back to the beginning of the sum to put a tick above each 23 as she added it to her running total. She checked some of her totals for accuracy as she worked.

Erin was keen to find as many totals as possible and would have carried on working much longer had the activity not drawn to a close. She understood that her objective was to find as many different totals as she could. She kept this in mind as a general working principle rather than keeping an ongoing specific check although, towards the end of her working time, she went back to check if she had replicated any totals. When she came across two sums with the same answer, rather than eliminate one of the sums, she decided to *'add another 4 and that'll make it a different total'* (see sums 4 and 6).

Erin identified several approaches to the task and adopted most of them. She showed persistence and found ways of overcoming challenges in her work, such as losing her place in repeated addition. She dealt efficiently with two matching totals, without having to abandon any previous efforts. Her work was clearly presented and showed organisation in parts. Erin was starting to check her work, although this was not yet consistent, as reflected by inaccuracies in the calculations. She was happy to discuss her work and gave a clear explanation of how she was using the number square to support addition of larger numbers. She showed a good understanding of the activity and was able to meet the task set. There is evidence of aspects of work at Level 3 in AT1 in this piece of work. However, to be more secure within the level, Erin would need to begin to develop a more systematically organised approach to her problem solving, such as is beginning to appear in the extracts from **Bella's** work below.

Bella demonstrated the beginnings of a more systematic approach to the task, though she has yet to become consistent in this.

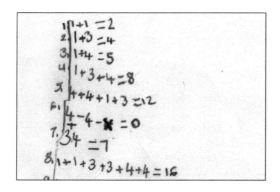

Number puzzles

Activity

Sending a letter

MATHEMATICAL CONTEXT

Ma2 Number
- Understanding addition and using related vocabulary; recognising that addition can be done in any order (Ma2/3a).
- Choosing sensible calculation methods to solve whole-number problems (including problems involving money), drawing on their understanding of the operations (Ma2/4a).
- Checking that their answers are reasonable and explaining their methods or reasoning (Ma2/4b).

ASSESSMENT OBJECTIVES

During this task, you may be able to observe whether the pupils can:

Problem solving
- approach problems involving number in order to identify what they need to do (Ma2/1a);
- develop flexible approaches to problem solving and look for ways to overcome difficulties (Ma2/1b);

Communicating
- use the correct language and vocabulary associated with number (Ma2/1e);
- communicate their findings in spoken, pictorial and written form (Ma2/1f);

Reasoning
- present results in an organised way (Ma2/1g);
- explain their methods and reasoning (Ma2/1i).

Materials needed
- A selection of coins of the appropriate value to support pupils if appropriate
- Resources for recording the outcome of the task (i.e. paper and pencil or paper 'stamps' of the appropriate value that can be cut out and stuck on)

A brief outline
Pupils explore ways of using stamps of different values to make a given total.

The activity

1 Introduce the task

Explain that you want to send a letter to a friend. It will cost 27p. You have stamps of the following values – 1p, 2p, 5p and 10p. Ask the pupils: 'How many different ways can you find of using the stamps to make 27p?' The value given for sending the letter could be lower, if necessary, so that pupils can better demonstrate their AT1 skills.

2 Work through the task

- Tell the pupils that their task is to find as many different ways as they can of making the given total using the numbers they have. You may wish to ask: 'How many ways do you think there might be?'

Mathematical Minds Key Stage 1

- Some pupils may be able to begin working independently at this point – observe them as they work and question them as you feel appropriate.
- Some pupils may need additional prompting, such as 'How are you going to find out?', 'Do you need anything to help you?', 'How are you going to show what you find out?' Note this as part of your observations.
- Make a note of any discussions the pupils have or explanations they give while they work.
- It may be useful to make coins of the same values available to pupils for whom this would be helpful. It is important to remember that, although this assessment can also tell you a lot about a pupil's understanding of money, its focus is on problem-solving skills.

Guidance on assessment and examples of pupils' work

Example 1: Sarah

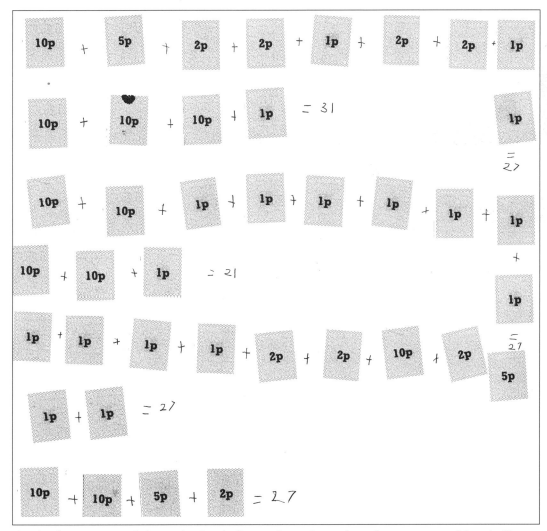

At the beginning of the task, Sarah focused on the task and concentrated hard. She asked several questions to clarify what the task entailed and then summarised: *'So I have to make 27 using the numbers on the stamps'*. She recognised that she should be using the process of addition and discussed her work in appropriate related terms. However, while observing Sarah working, it became clear that she found the actual mechanics of addition a challenge at times. The main approach she adopted seemed to be to select larger value stamps to start with and then 'build up' to 27 with smaller value stamps. This strategy proved successful on most occasions where she remembered the task set. However, as the second and fourth sums show, she occasionally lost sight of the focus of the task. In these instances she was observed to pick up a random selection of stamps and calculate the total they made. She was often asked: 'How much did we say the letter would cost to send?' in order to help her refocus on the task set.

Sarah made a good attempt to present her results in a clear and organised manner. Her system broke down when working with sums where the layout exceeded the width of the page. She was clear in her own mind as to how these layouts worked, explaining orally. However, she could not really see that it might be confusing for others reading her work. She made the decision to set them out like a sum *'to help show they need adding up to make 27'*.

Sarah was demonstrating some elements of Level 2 in AT1 on this piece of work: she selected appropriate mathematics to use, although she struggled with the actual application. When discussing her work she used appropriate language and she presented it with symbols and numbers. However, Sarah found it difficult to remain focused on the task without support. She was not yet able to see any relationships between the numbers involved, such as 10 being equal to two lots of 5 independently, and even with prompting she was not able to use this to support her work. These aspects of her work on this task were judged to be more indicative of Level 1.

Example 2: Kirsten

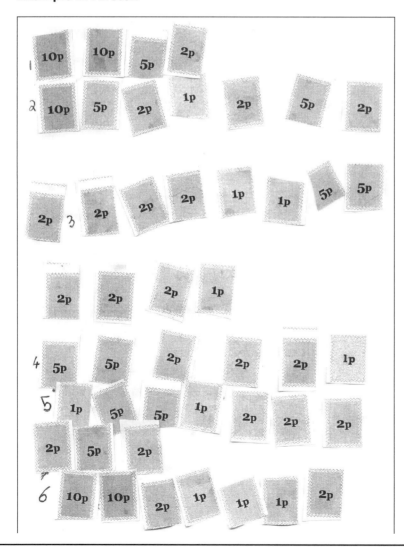

Mathematical Minds Key Stage 1

Example 2: Kirsten *continued*

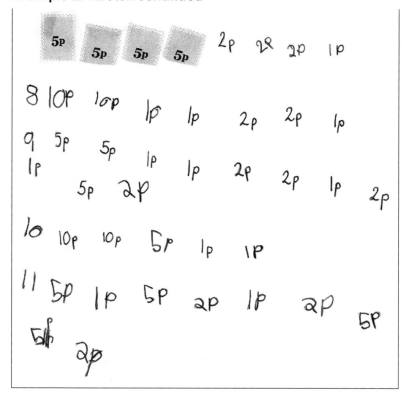

Kirsten began work quickly, demonstrating a clear understanding of her task. She worked confidently with numbers and addition strategies, using appropriate vocabulary in discussing her work. Through observation, she seemed to be beginning to use the relationships between numbers in her working (i.e. 10 is equal to 5 and 5, or 2 and 2 and 2 and 2 and 2), although she was not explicit about this strategy when asked. There is evidence that, as her work progressed, she began to alternate between two main ways of working. The first of these was to experiment with ways of making 20p and keeping the 7p element simple (5 and 2, or 5 and 1 and 1). The second was to keep the 20p element simpler (10 and 10, or four 5s) and explore ways of making 7p. This strategy was in greater evidence in the second part of her work, after a more random investigation to start with.

Kirsten made a good attempt at organising and presenting her work clearly, setting her work out in rows and numbering each group of stamps that made up one 'sum'. On the whole she checked her work carefully, making only two errors (see sums 4 and 11). However, she was not yet working in a methodical way that would make it easier to keep track of combinations already used and this led to some replication of sums.

Kirsten showed evidence that she was beginning to explore different approaches to solving the problem, although she was not able to explain her thinking. She used appropriate mathematical language in conversations about her work, and she represented her work pictorially. She showed evidence of organisation in her work, but did not check her work at an appropriate level. There is clearly some evidence of Level 3 attainment in AT1 in this piece of work but, to demonstrate secure Level 3 attainment, Kirsten would have needed to explain her reasoning and problem-solving strategies in more depth, and shown a more methodical approach.

Example 3: Safina

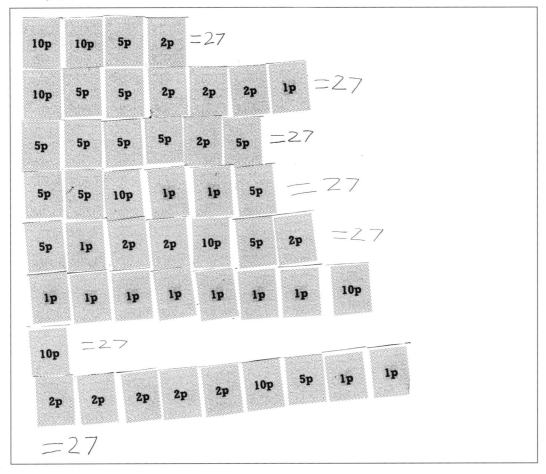

Initially, Safina approached the task in a systematic manner, stating: *'I'm going to start with the simplest way of doing it, then I'm going to use more and more numbers'*. As Safina worked practically with the stamps, she was observed to be very organised and started with the largest number each time. Unfortunately, some of this rigour was lost when she recorded her work on paper.

Safina was clearly confident with number, which she used to good effect as a strategy to solve this problem. She was overheard discussing with another pupil how the use of multiples could help them: *'... five 5s are 25, so we could do that then just add another 2 somehow to make 27'*. She then asked her friend: *'How many 2s are in 27?'* When questioned, she explained that she knew 27 was an odd number so it would not be a direct multiple of 2, but she was thinking of how many 2p stamps she would need to go with a 1p stamp. Like Kirsten, Safina also investigated the problem by expanding on either the 20p or the 7p element. In some cases she also broke the amount down further into 10, 10 and 7 and expanded one of the 10s as well as the 7. Safina had thought through and vocalised her approach to the problem. She was unable to work through the problem to a satisfactory resolution in her eyes, but this was due to time constraints rather than to her not appreciating the full potential of the task. She organised and checked her work both for replications and for accuracy.

Safina was judged to be working securely within Level 3 in AT1 on this task.

Mathematical Minds Key Stage 1

Activity

The new front door

MATHEMATICAL CONTEXT

Ma3 Shape, space and measures
- Recognising simple spatial patterns and relationships and making predictions about them (Ma3/1e).
- Recognising reflective symmetry in familiar 2-D shapes and patterns (Ma3/2d).

ASSESSMENT OBJECTIVES

During this task, you may be able to observe whether the pupils can:

Problem solving
- try different approaches and find ways of overcoming difficulties when solving shape and space problems (Ma3/1a);

Reasoning
- recognise simple spatial patterns and relationships and make predictions about them (Ma3/1e);
- use mathematical communication and explanation skills (Ma3/1f).

Materials needed
- Plenty of multi-link (or similar resource cubes/squares) in two colours for each pupil
- Means of recording outcomes (e.g. coloured pencils, squared paper or a recording sheet, camera)

A brief outline
Pupils explore the number of ways in which two colours can be used to create a range of patterns.

The activity

1 Introduce the task

Explain that Mr and Mrs Rainbow are getting a new front door. They cannot decide on one colour, so have agreed to have two colours. To make it fair, they have decided to each paint half of the front door with their chosen colour. This is what their new front door will look like before it is painted. (Draw this on the board, or similar.)

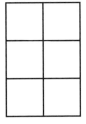

The pupils' task is to help them decide how to paint it, by showing all the different designs they could have. They can use multi-link cubes to help them think up their designs, but must remember that they can only use *two* colours and the shape must stay the same as the original door.

2 Work through the task

- Having explained the task, either allow pupils to choose six cubes (with three of each colour), or provide this for them as a starting point.
- Remind the pupils that they must stick to the two colours they have and keep the door shape, but that they can move the cubes around within this shape to make different patterns.

- The pupils can record their designs by colouring door shapes on squared paper or a recording sheet, or photographs could be taken of the different designs and kept as evidence.
- Observe the pupils as they work and discuss their work with them as you feel appropriate. Make a note of any discussions the pupils have or explanations they give while they work.

Guidance on assessment and examples of pupils' work

Pupils originally worked in colour for this activity. Colour has been replaced by shading in the images of pupils' work presented below.

Example 1: Leon

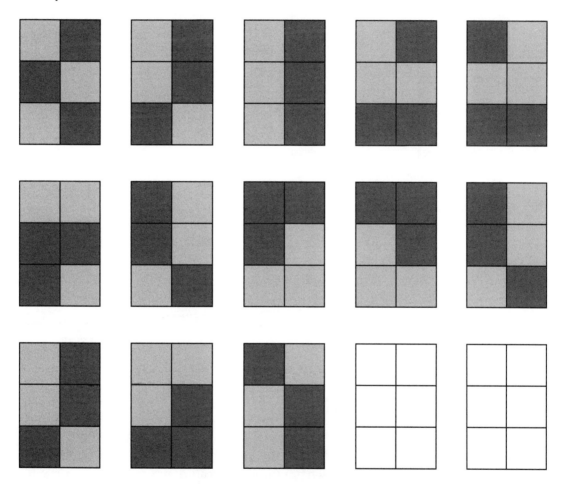

Leon settled to the task with much enthusiasm. After selecting his two colours of cubes, he put them together in a random fashion to create his first design, which he reproduced on the recording sheet. He then disassembled this design and randomly made another (shown in 'door 2'). This process continued after each design had been recorded and he diligently referred back to his sheet each time to check: *'Have I done this one yet?'* He continued to generate a range of designs in a random fashion and recorded his work clearly on the sheet. He was happy to explain his work and used positional language in describing his patterns.

In this activity Leon was judged to be working confidently within Level 1 in AT1, although the mathematical language he used was more akin to expectations of Level 2 performance.

Example 2: Oliver

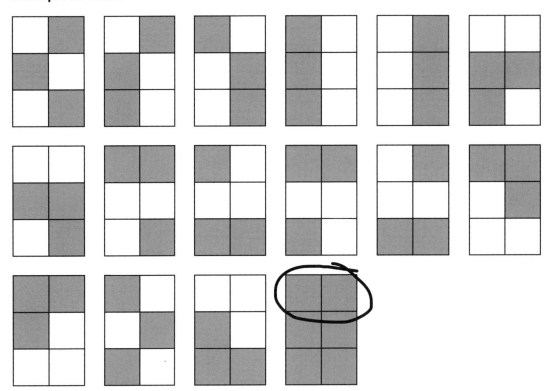

When the task was explained to him, Oliver's immediate reaction was: *'Well I'm going to choose black and white as my colours then I only have to do half the colouring in!'* He selected his cubes and assembled them as shown in the first 'door'. He then swapped the position of the two bottom cubes to make another design. As he was about to rearrange the cubes again he said *'Hey, all I need to do is make a pattern and then do the opposite each time'*. With that, he turned over the block of cubes and reproduced this new arrangement in 'door 3'.

He then abandoned the cubes and continued working visually. Designs 2 to 7 demonstrated Oliver's systematic approach, in that they show a pattern that is reflected through a vertical axis to create a new pattern. However, at this point, his pace of work slowed as he found himself recreating patterns which he had already used. He then actually began to reflect previously used patterns through horizontal axes, although he did not appear to be aware of this transformation, merely considering it *'a new design'*. As he reached the bottom of the page, he became more distracted and his systematic approach appeared to break down as he found himself beginning to replicate previous designs. He tried various designs but ended up with all the squares coloured in and no legible answer.

He worked enthusiastically and was happy to explain what he was doing in simple terms, such as 'opposite' and 'reversing it'.

Oliver recognised some symmetry in his pattern work and used this to great effect to enable him to complete the task efficiently. He was able to explain his work, recognising that some sets of doors were 'opposites', although was not yet using specific, appropriate vocabulary such as 'reflection' or 'line of symmetry' in his discussions of how he created the patterns. He quickly developed a very systematic and efficient mode of working, drawing on a variety of approaches to solving the problem (swapping cubes, reflecting designs, just drawing). This enabled him to create and present his patterns in an organised way, making good use of the given method of recording. On the basis of this evidence, Oliver was deemed to be working quite confidently at Level 3 in AT1 in this piece of work.

Mathematics levels

Attainment target 1: Using and applying mathematics

Teachers should expect attainment at a given level in this attainment target to be demonstrated through activities in which the mathematics from the other attainment targets is at, or very close to, the same level.

Level 1

Pupils use mathematics as an integral part of classroom activities. They represent their work with objects or pictures and discuss it. They recognise and use a simple pattern or relationship.

Level 2

Pupils select the mathematics they use in some classroom activities. They discuss their work using mathematical language and are beginning to represent it using symbols and simple diagrams. They explain why an answer is correct.

Level 3

Pupils try different approaches and find ways of overcoming difficulties that arise when they are solving problems. They are beginning to organise their work and check results. Pupils discuss their mathematical work and are beginning to explain their thinking. They use and interpret mathematical symbols and diagrams. Pupils show that they understand a general statement by finding particular examples that match it.

Level 4

Pupils are developing their own strategies for solving problems and are using these strategies both in working within mathematics and in applying mathematics to practical contexts. They present information and results in a clear and organised way. They search for a solution by trying out ideas of their own.

Level 5

In order to carry through tasks and solve mathematical problems, pupils identify and obtain necessary information. They check their results, considering whether these are sensible. Pupils show understanding of situations by describing them mathematically using symbols, words and diagrams. They draw simple conclusions of their own and give an explanation of their reasoning.

Level 6

Pupils carry through substantial tasks and solve quite complex problems by independently breaking them down into smaller, more manageable tasks. They interpret, discuss and synthesise information presented in a variety of mathematical forms. Pupils' writing explains and informs their use of diagrams. Pupils are beginning to give mathematical justifications.

Level 7

Starting from problems or contexts that have been presented to them, pupils progressively refine or extend the mathematics used to generate fuller solutions. They give a reason for their choice of mathematical presentation, explaining features they have selected. Pupils justify their generalisations, arguments or solutions, showing some insight into the mathematical structure of the problem. They appreciate the difference between mathematical explanation and experimental evidence.

Level 8

Pupils develop and follow alternative approaches. They reflect on their own lines of enquiry when exploring mathematical tasks; in doing so they introduce and use a range of mathematical techniques. Pupils convey mathematical or statistical meaning through precise and consistent use of symbols that is sustained throughout the work. They examine generalisations or solutions reached in an activity, commenting constructively on the reasoning and logic or the process employed, or the results obtained, and make further progress in the activity as a result.

Exceptional performance

Pupils give reasons for the choices they make when investigating within mathematics itself or when using mathematics to analyse tasks; these reasons explain why particular lines of enquiry or procedures are followed and others rejected. Pupils apply the mathematics they know in familiar and unfamiliar contexts. Pupils use mathematical language and symbols effectively in presenting a convincing reasoned argument. Their reports include mathematical justifications, explaining their solutions to problems involving a number of features or variables.

Department for Education and Employment and Qualifications Authority (1999) *The National Curriculum for England: Key Stages 1–4*. London: HMSO.